Desserts

and Sweet Snacks

Desserts

and
Sweet Snacks

Rustic

Italian Style

Viana La Place

photographs by Deborah Jones

William Morrow and Company, Inc.   New York

It is the policy of William Morrow and Company, Inc., and its imprints and affiliates, recognizing the importance of preserving what has been written, to print the books we publish on acid-free paper, and we exert our best efforts to that end.

Library of Congress Cataloging-in-Publication Data

La Place, Viana.
  Desserts and sweet snacks: rustic Italian style/Viana La Place; photographs by Deborah Jones
    p. cm.
  Includes index.
  ISBN 0-688-14139-0 (hardcover)
  1. Desserts—Italy. 2. Cookery, Italian. I. Title.
  TX773.L297 1998
  641.8'6'0945—dc21   97-44586
                      CIP

Printed in the United States of America

First Edition

1   2   3   4   5   6   7   8   9   10

Book design by Richard Oriolo

www.williammorrow.com

Acknowledgments

Sincerest thanks to a group of wonderful and talented people: Deborah Jones, for always pushing to get the truest photograph; Jeri Jones, for providing invaluable assistance to Deborah; Sandra Cook, a food stylist with a caring and sensitive touch; Allyson Levy, her trusty assistant who always helped me in my kitchen in the final days of completing this project; and Sara Slavin, stylist and all-around great human being. As always, Sonia Greenbaum copyedited this book with keen attention to detail. Finally, thank you to all of my Italian friends who have inspired me over the years.

Contents

Introduction

The recipes in this book take their inspiration from a number of sources, but Italy, and always Italy, informs the spirit of the book. Whether that inspiration is drawn from home cooks making magic with pantry staples or the fun fantasies of sidewalk caffè creations, an Italian sensibility is always present.

Italians are famous for their sweet tooth and the elaborate nature of desserts created to feed it. In fact, in Italy there exists a parallel universe of sweets created by home cooks. These are more earthbound, simpler affairs that transform basic ingredients into truly great desserts through artistry, imagination, and skill: rice into a superb rice cake; semolina into a dense, creamy pudding; ricotta into a rich chocolate cream. These are the desserts I make at home, the ones I crave, that I find even more beautiful than many of the more involved creations that appear in pastry shop windows.

Most of the recipes here take their cue from this home style of dessert. These are everyday creations, ones you'll want to make over and over again, wholesome and fresh.

Homespun is a word that describes them, but they have an innate elegance and always a touch of fantasy. And in keeping with my "less is more" philosophy about kitchen equipment and techniques, the fanciest equipment you'll need is a hand-held beater to whip egg whites and cream, and an inexpensive ice cream machine.

Italy informs both the choice of ingredients and the style and manner in which they are prepared and served. I have not included in the pages of this book any French-inspired pastries, nor will you find recipes for American-style cakes and pies. Instead, I share with you the pleasures of desserts that reflect the simplicity and restraint of traditional *cucina casareccia*, Italian home cooking: single-layer cakes "frosted" with only a dusting of powdered sugar, a crostata with a thin layer of luscious pastry cream and a topping of melon slices, a wine-rich sweet cherry bruschetta.

Appropriateness is another word that comes to mind when I think about the Italian approach to sweets. After a carefully cooked and balanced meal, a rich dessert is inappropriate. In fact, most Italian meals at home end with fruit of the season, which not only refreshes and sweetens the mouth and ends the meal on a leisurely note but also keeps one at the table for the time it takes for digestion to begin. Fruits are full of goodness, but are not eaten out of duty. Watching an Italian eat fruit at the end of a meal leaves no doubt as to the intense pleasure being experienced. A bowl of summer cherries or peaches, or a plate of ripe figs, winter pears, or fall persimmons, satisfies that natural craving for sweetness.

To this end, I've included an abundance of dessert recipes in which fruits are kept as close to their natural state as possible. You'll be amazed at how much pleasure you can derive from beautiful, ripe fruits bathed in honeyed Moscato or sprinkled lightly with Maraschino liqueur or fragrant rose water.

Of couse, Italians do indulge in sweets of an almost baroque complexity, but rarely after a meal. More often than not, pastries are taken in the afternoon, along with an espresso at a caffè or coffee bar, as a pick-me-up between lunch and dinner, which often isn't eaten until nine o'clock at night.

Italians also go to the corner *pasticceria*, pastry shop, to purchase more elaborate creations, and offer them to family and friends with absolutely no pretense of having prepared them themselves. In Italy, buying pastries or bread from artisans specially trained in their craft is the norm, and no stigma is attached to it, no sense of failure or compromise at having not prepared them oneself. To me, this reflects a more communal spirit, as opposed to our pioneer tradition of needing to do everything oneself.

Stops at the *gelateria* for ice cream and granita can occur almost any time of the day or night, but ice cream and ices are rarely served at the end of a meal. I've included recipes for a few ice cream fantasies inspired by Italian caffè traditions, and a whipped cream–filled brioche that might be offered at a caffè, but I view them more as treats enjoyed on a summer afternoon than desserts served at the end of a meal.

Many of the recipes in this book make healthy and substantial snacks perfect for satisfying those afternoon cravings: a piece of Semolina Cake, Baked Apple with Italian Pudding, or Quince Fruit Candies. Some of the desserts can even be served as breakfast, such as Sweet Olive Oil Quick Bread, Warm Apple Panino, and Ricotta with Honey and Almonds. A certain flexibility is built into the desserts, making them suitable for serving any time of the day.

Desserts are an invitation to the sensual world. They mean giving in to pleasure, losing oneself in the moment. But sensuality does not have to be equated with richness, as is so often the case. Nothing is more sensual than a ripe, fragrant peach or plump sweet dates filled with creamy ricotta scented with orange blossom water. A simple slice of country bread and a piece of dark chocolate, my very favorite afternoon treat, feels wonderfully indulgent and satisfying; it is utterly seductive, but there is a wholesomeness at its core that keeps it in the realm of what I would call real food.

Sweets play a special role in the foods that we eat. They are inextricably linked to a moment, an experience, a time of day, a season—they enter the world of memory and fantasy. A drift of whipped cream dotted with blackberries reminds us of summer. A taste of melon ice cream can take you back to a particular coffee bar in a small Italian town by the sea.

Desserts can be ethereal, such as melt-in-your-mouth, warm Ricotta Soufflé, or more substantial, such as Sweet Spaghettini Torta, to name only two. Desserts can also enter our dreams—the dark, bittersweet flavors of Espresso Cake linger on in our minds long after the taste has vanished.

It is pleasure that is at the heart of this book, pure sensory pleasure. That was my touchstone—recipes that provide moments of magical delight. My hope is that this book guides you not only to the preparation of various delicious desserts and snacks, but also to a greater awareness of a way of eating that will enhance your daily lives.

Simple Offerings

Rough Bread with Wine and Sugar

A quick, rough snack or dessert that satisfies one's hunger immediately. All you need are some good rustic bread, a bit of sugar, and some strong red wine. **Makes 1 serving**

1 thick slice country bread

Full-bodied red wine

Sugar

Place the bread on a plate and splash with enough wine to moisten the bread. Sprinkle generously with sugar. Knives and forks are irrelevant here. This is best eaten by bringing the bread to your mouth with your hand.

Acaya Dessert

The scene: Acaya, a small town in Puglia during a cold, dark winter season. It is the lunch hour, and the streets are desolate except for a few mangy dogs running free and a solitary boy on a bicycle. A handful of cars are parked in front of the restaurant in Acaya that is our destination. We rush from the car to the restaurant, where it is warm and inviting.

Our lunch, an amazing succession of small tastes brought to us, one after another, on diminutive platters, left little room for the sweets offered. It was a bowl of oranges, tangerines, and fresh fennel wedges placed on the table that provided the perfect bright, clean, refreshing ending to our meal.

Makes 2 to 3 servings

1 medium or 2 small fennel bulbs

2 oranges

3 tangerines

Trim the base of the fennel bulb and cut off the feathery top. Remove the coarse outer layer of the bulb. Cut the bulb into eighths lengthwise. Arrange the fennel in a bowl or basket lined with a clean cloth napkin along with washed oranges and tangerines. Provide forks and knives for the fruit.

Desserts and Sweet Snacks

Bread and Chocolate

Good bread and dark chocolate. Ever since I was a child, this elemental combination has been my favorite sweet snack.

Together, they are wholesome and sensual. Nourishing and seductive. There is an exciting balance of flavor——the bittersweetness of the chocolate, its restrained richness, tempered by the warm, nutty taste of bread. And there is the melting sensation on the tongue of the chocolate merging with the bread.

A slice of country bread topped with a few squares of chocolate broken off a chocolate bar, or a little chocolate sandwich, satisfies me completely——any time of the day or night. **Makes 1 serving**

1½ ounces bittersweet chocolate, approximately

1 to 2 small slices country bread

Place 1 or 2 squares of chocolate on a slice of bread about the same size as the chocolate, or slide chocolate squares between 2 slices of bread. Serve as a snack or as a very rustic dessert.

Fruit Bowl Lido San Giovanni

Summer on the Mediterranean. I spent a lazy July doing not much more than taking daily swims in the sea. The heat was so intense that, other than shuffling around my apartment in a groggy stupor, normal activity was just about impossible. Often I'd have lunch at the beach, too, then return to my umbrella and lounge chair to spend the rest of the afternoon hoping for any merciful cooling breeze that the sea might offer up.

Most of my lunches at the trattoria at Lido San Giovanni would end with a selection of ripe, fragrant fruits, brought in a small glass bowl with a little water in the bottom and a few ice cubes, to keep the fruit cool and moist. **Makes 2 to 3 servings**

1 small green-skinned pear

Small handful white-fleshed cherries

1 fragrant peach

1 large kiwi

Ice cubes

Place the fruits in a bowl. Add ice cubes and a drizzle of water. Use a knife and fork to peel and slice fruits.

Sweet Mineral Juices

Sweet Mineral Juices Although one normally thinks of ending a meal with a dessert or fruit, southern Italians sometimes finish with crisp vegetables known to aid digestion and refresh the mouth.

Any individual vegetable can be served, or you can serve a combination. Crisp, juicy celery stalks, sweet fennel, and the pale, tender inner leaves of chicory or escarole go well together. Or offer a simple plate of fresh, tender romaine lettuce leaves.

Celery

Fennel

Escarole or chicory

1 tender head romaine lettuce

Select a head of celery that has many tender inner stalks. Remove the tough outer stalks of the celery for another use. Serve the tender inner stalks without trimming away the leafy tops. Celery leaves are tender and have a bracing, herbal flavor.

Small to medium-size fennel bulbs are the most tender and have fewer developed fibrous strings. Trim away the top of the fennel bulb and remove the outer layer if it is very tough and discolored. Cut the bulb in half, then cut into slim wedges.

Remove the dark green outer leaves of escarole and reserve them for another use. The small, tender, pale yellow inner leaves can be served whole.

Select a small head of romaine lettuce. Large heads tend to have tough, somewhat bitter leaves. Discard any outer leaves that are discolored and damaged. Tender and unblemished leaves can be served whole.

EATING CANTALOUPE
BY THE SEA

By the pure, clean waters of the Adriatic, way down in the heel of the Italian boot, I had the best bowl of steamed mussels I've ever eaten.

The open-air restaurant, really no more than a stand with tables and benches protected from the sun by a latticed cane roof, was sitting right on the rocky coastline. The proprietor was a rough-looking fisherman with a gold necklace, a weathered face, and a sweet, generous personality. Below the "shack," down by the rocks and immersed in the sea, were beds of mussels gathered as needed.

Those mussels tasted so good, eaten at the source, with the briny scent of the sea in the air. And what did I have for dessert? A whole cantaloupe, handed to me along with a knife. It doesn't get more rustic than that!

Warm Apple Panino

Just one bite of this rustic sandwich will win you over completely. The wholesome combination of good bread and fresh-cooked apple slices, with minimal sugar and a few simple embellishments, ends up tasting like apple pie. Quick and easy to prepare, the panino makes a great afternoon snack that satisfies a craving for something sweet. **Makes 1 serving**

1 medium oblong roll, split, or 2 slices crusty bread

Unsalted butter

Apricot preserves

½ apple

1 teaspoon sugar

A few drops lemon juice

Pull out some of the inside of the bread roll to create a hollow in the top and bottom halves of the roll. Butter the top half of the roll and spread the bottom half with the apricot preserves. Toast the slices, butter and preserves side up, for about 10 minutes at 350°F, or place briefly under the broiler until the bread is a little browned around the edges.

Meanwhile, peel and core the apple half and thinly slice lengthwise. In a skillet over medium-high heat, sauté the apple slices in ½ tablespoon butter, adding the sugar and lemon juice. When the apple slices are tender but still hold their shape, 3 to 4 minutes, pile the slices in the bottom half of the roll and cover with the top half. Press down on the sandwich to flatten it a little bit. Eat the sandwich warm.

Sweet Bruschetta with Mascarpone

I explored the idea of sweet bruschettas in my book *Panini, Bruschetta, Crostini*, and continue to be intrigued by the possibilities.

Here's a new version of sweet bruschetta; it's as simple as can be, but incredibly good. Purchase high-quality orange marmalade in specialty food stores. **Makes 1 serving**

1 slice crusty bread

Orange marmalade

Mascarpone

Toast the bread. Spread with a thin layer of orange marmalade. Then top with as much or as little mascarpone as you like.

Fresh Fruit Desserts

FRUIT FOR DESSERT

My mother tells me that her grandmother could not sit down at the

dinner table unless there was a bowl of fresh fruit placed at its cen-

ter, so crucial was this part of the meal.

Today, we emphasize the importance of eating fresh fruit.

Why not perform the simple act of placing a bowl of carefully

selected washed fruits on the table before sitting down to eat?

Fruits bring a meal to a satisfying close. Their sweet flavor

and refreshing juices cleanse the mouth, leaving a fresh, sweet

sensation on the tongue. Their perfumes and colors bring pleasure

to our senses. The slow pace of eating fruits——peeling, cutting

into slices, the journey to the mouth——allows the meal to end

on a leisurely note, promoting both conversation and digestion!

For special dinners, offer pieces of dark chocolate and whole

almonds along with the fruit. In my opinion, there is no more

perfect way to end a meal.

Fresh Figs with Chocolate and Almond Stuffing

A version of this combination, divinely good, made its first appearance in *Unplugged Kitchen*. But like a zealot, I share it here because I want everyone to experience its pleasures.

Makes 12 stuffed figs

¾ cup finely chopped, unpeeled almonds

2 ounces finely chopped semisweet chocolate, about ½ cup

1 tablespoon sugar

1½ tablespoons dark rum or enough to lightly bind almonds and chocolate into a paste

12 ripe, juicy figs

Place the almonds, chocolate, and sugar in a bowl and stir together. Add the rum and stir until the mixture just holds together. Add a few more drops of rum as needed. It should form a rough-textured paste. if it doesn't hold together, pound mixture in a mortar and pestle or pulse briefly in a blender.

Trim the stems off the figs. Starting at the stem end, cut the figs ¾ of the way down, making two incisions in the form of a cross. Carefully pinch the bottom of each fig to make the top open like a flower.

Gently stuff the almond mixture into the center of each fig. Press the fig together to reshape it. Arrange figs on a platter and serve. On a warm day, keep figs refrigerated until ready to serve. To be eaten with the fingers.

Blood Oranges in Orange Liqueur

It was early spring and I'd decided to go on a bus tour that circled the coast of Sicily. There were only eight passengers on that big plush bus: an architect whose ballerina wife was performing in Palermo, a Bolivian man and his mother, two English ladies, a Canadian dentist and his wife, and me.

It rained quite a bit, lovely spring rain, giving a light sheen to all the Greek ruins we visited. Wildflowers were in bloom—red poppies and blue borage, and yellow mountain fennel as tall as me. At that time of year we seemed to be the only tour bus on the road and had the island all to ourselves.

My only regret was that I didn't get to taste the blood oranges flavored with orange liqueur listed on the menu posted outside that little restaurant in Siracusa, just across from the church we were visiting. But our time was up in that beautiful town by the sea and the tour bus was ready to depart for its next destination. **Makes 6 servings**

Desserts and Sweet Snacks

10 blood oranges

6 tablespoons sugar or to taste

Juice of $\frac{1}{2}$ medium lemon

3 to 4 tablespoons Cointreau

Peel 8 oranges, cutting away all the white pith and membranes. Cut the oranges horizontally into thin slices about $\frac{3}{8}$ inch thick. Pick out the seeds. Layer the slices in a shallow serving bowl. Sprinkle with sugar. Squeeze the juice from the remaining oranges and pour it, with the lemon juice, over the orange slices. Carefully turn the oranges over in the juices a few times. Cover and refrigerate for a few hours.

Before serving, drizzle the liqueur over the top and turn the slices over in the juices once or twice. Serve chilled.

Chocolate Peaches

An extra-chocolaty version of a classic Italian dessert——baked peaches filled with amaretti cookies and almonds. Grated lemon rind adds a fragrant, citrus fruit note to the deep chocolate flavor. **Makes 4 servings**

4 large peaches

½ cup sugar

Grated zest of 1 lemon

4 pairs (8 individual) amaretti cookies, crushed

¼ cup peeled and chopped almonds

2 tablespoons Dutch-process dark cocoa

1 egg yolk

2 tablespoons unsalted butter

Dip the peaches very briefly in boiling water. Peel and cut the peaches in half, following the natural division line of the fruit. Remove the pits. Arrange the peach halves in a baking dish. Scoop out a little flesh from each peach to enlarge the cavity and reserve.

Preheat the oven to 350°F.

In a bowl, combine ¼ cup of the sugar, the lemon zest, crushed amaretti, almonds, and cocoa. Stir together. Add the reserved peach flesh and the egg yolk, and stir until well blended. You should end up with a thick paste. If it is too thick, add a little more peach flesh and juice, scooped out from the peach cavities.

Divide the mixture among the peaches, filling the cavity of each peach. Top with shavings of butter and generously sprinkle with the remaining sugar.

Bake for 25 minutes, or until the filling is firm and has formed a crust, and the peaches are tender but still hold their shape.

Blackberries and Panna

A classic Italian approach to berries and cream. Dark, luscious blackberries are held in suspension in a dense cloud of *panna,* freshly whipped cream.

Makes 6 servings

4 cups ripe blackberries

¼ cup plus 2 tablespoons sugar

1 cup heavy cream

To clean the berries, gently dip a few at a time into a bowl of cool water and carefully lift out. Drain well on paper towels. Transfer to a shallow bowl. Sprinkle with ¼ cup sugar. Chill until needed.

In a bowl, whip the cream with the remaining 2 tablespoons sugar until thick and fluffy. Whipped cream can be refrigerated for several hours. Whip again very briefly before using.

Just before serving, add berries, a few at a time, to the whipped cream, gently folding the berries in without crushing them. Spoon into serving bowls or goblets. Serve immediately.

Peaches in a Glass of Red Wine

Hot, hot summer by the Mediterranean. Evening has come but it's still too hot to think, to move. In the apartment buildings across the street, families are eating on their terraces, and I can hear them talk and hear the clink of dishes and glasses, can smell the fragrant tomato sauce that's been cooking.

I'm eating a peach cut up into tiny dice spooned into a tumbler, with homemade red wine from a friend filling all the little spaces left by the peach. The wine is rose-colored, fresh and light, so different from store-bought wines. This wine just makes you happy, not drunk——and never gives you a headache. And to sweeten the fruit, I add a few wine-soaked sugar cubes and crush them against the side of the glass. **Makes 1 serving**

1 peach, unpeeled

Chilled light red wine or rosé

2 to 3 sugar cubes

Cut the peach into small dice, about ¼ inch. Spoon into a tall glass. Pour enough wine in the glass to cover the diced peaches. Add the sugar cubes. Wait a few seconds as the sugar absorbs the wine. Then crush the cubes against the side of the glass with a spoon, and stir a little.

Raspberries in Moscato Wine

Dessert wine made from Moscato grapes has a honeyed flavor and flowery, orange blossom bouquet. The perfume alone is enough to make you swoon. Its effect on raspberries is magical.

Raspberries are a very fragile fruit. If left in their little basket, they become moldy rather quickly. When you bring raspberries home from the market, take them out of the container and spread them out on a plate. This helps extend their life and keeps them intact. **Makes 4 to 5 servings**

2 baskets ripe raspberries

1 to 2 tablespoons sugar, depending on the sweetness of the berries

½ cup chilled Moscato di Pantelleria or Asti Spumante

Lightly rinse the raspberries to remove dust. Drain on a clean dish cloth or paper towel. Sprinkle with sugar to taste and gently turn raspberries over once or twice with a spoon.

Mound the raspberries in individual dessert goblets and cover with cold wine. Serve immediately.

Summer Fruits with Rose Water and Lemon

A summer garden of rose and lemon essences heightens the flavor of fresh, luscious fruit. Serve this fruit dessert cold, on a very hot day. Just before bringing the fruit to the table, stir in a few ice cubes and whole mint leaves to further refresh the senses.

And if you have some unsprayed roses in your garden, and are in a completely sybaritic mood, sprinkle some rose petals over the top of the fruit. **Makes 4 servings**

½ cantaloupe, diced

½ honeydew, diced

3 peeled peaches or 3 unpeeled nectarines, diced

¼ cup sugar

2 teaspoons lemon juice and a strip of lemon peel, yellow part only

2 tablespoons rose water

Ice cubes

Whole mint leaves

Rose petals (only if they haven't been sprayed with chemicals), optional

Gently place the fruits in a serving bowl. Sprinkle with sugar and add lemon juice and peel. Cover and chill for 30 minutes, stirring once or twice. Add the rose water and chill another 30 minutes.

To serve, stir in ice cubes and mint leaves, and sprinkle with optional rose petals. I don't recommend eating the mint leaves or rose petals.

Pink Grapefruit Dessert

Grapefruit has a clear, keen taste that makes it ideal at the end of a meal, especially after a seafood dinner. It refreshes the mouth perhaps better than any other fruit. Just looking at the glistening, jewellike pink flesh of ruby grapefruit is a cooling experience.

Instead of relegating it to the morning hours, try serving grapefruit as a dessert——with a sprinkle of sugar and a shot of Maraschino. This colorless potent liqueur with its hint of fresh cherry flavor seems to magically accentuate the flavor of almost any fruit. **Makes 2 servings**

2 large ruby red grapefruit
2 tablespoons Maraschino liqueur
2 tablespoons sugar

Cut the unpeeled grapefruit into eighths or sixteenths, depending on size of fruit. Working over a bowl, cut the grapefruit segments from the peel, making sure to remove all the white pith. Squeeze the peels over the bowl to extract any remaining juices. Sprinkle with Maraschino and sugar. Stir. Cover and chill until cool, or keep refrigerated for several hours. To serve, spoon fruit and juices into 2 small dessert goblets.

Watermelon and Chocolate

Here, crisp and refreshing watermelon is carefully seeded and diced, then topped with shavings of bittersweet chocolate. The watermelon, a pure deep pink with a dark shower of chocolate, looks beautiful, and the contrast of flavors is fascinating. **Makes 6 servings**

4 pounds ripe watermelon with rind

2 tablespoons sugar, optional

2 ounces bittersweet chocolate, shaved

Remove the rind from the watermelon, cutting away any part of the flesh that isn't sweet and ripe. Dice the melon and carefully pick out all seeds. If the watermelon is not intensely sweet, sprinkle with the optional sugar. Toss gently. Chill until needed.

Just before serving, spoon the watermelon and juices into chilled goblets and sprinkle chocolate shavings over the top.

Cherry Bruschetta

This dessert has all the rustic charm of a savory warm bruschetta. Cooking cherries in red wine and sugar is a time-honored tradition in Italy. Here, I use the wine-rich, cherry-sweet compote as a topping for sturdy country bread, toasted and spread with a touch of sweet butter. **Makes 4 servings**

¾ cup sugar or to taste

1 cup red wine

1 piece lemon rind

1½ pounds sweet cherries, pitted

4 thick slices country bread

1½ tablespoons unsalted butter

Combine the sugar, red wine, and lemon rind in a medium saucepan. Stir until the sugar dissolves. Add the cherries and stir. Bring to a boil over high heat, then reduce the heat to low and simmer, uncovered, for 15 minutes.

Lightly grill or toast the bread and spread with a little butter. Place the bread on 4 individual dessert plates. Spoon the cherries and their juices over the bread. Serve warm.

Baked Apples with Italian Pudding

Italians love baked apples, too. These are filled with a simple Italian pastry cream studded with rum-soaked currants and pine nuts.

Looking homespun but just a little fancy with their creamy pudding crowns, these apples are delicious served after a simple meal, as part of a brunch, or as a midnight snack. **Makes 6 servings**

FOR THE APPLES

6 Pippin apples or other variety appropriate for baking

Thin shavings of unsalted butter

¼ cup sugar

FOR THE FILLING

¼ cup currants

¼ cup pine nuts

¼ cup dark rum

1 tablespoon sugar

1 recipe Italian Pastry Cream (page 36)

Core the whole apples well and cut away some of the flesh to make a generous 1½-inch-wide well in the center. Make sure to keep the bottom intact.

Fill each apple with a shaving of butter and sprinkle with sugar. Bake at 350°F for 45 minutes to an hour, until the apples are tender but still hold their shape. Cool to room temperature.

continued

Meanwhile, place the currants in a sieve over a pot of boiling water and plump for about 5 minutes, or until they soften and swell up. In a small sauté pan over low heat, toast the pine nuts until light brown, stirring often, 6 to 8 minutes. Immediately transfer to a plate and let cool. Place the currants and pine nuts in a small bowl. Add rum and sugar, and stir briefly.

Prepare the pastry cream. Reserve about half for another use.

Drain the currants and pine nuts well, reserving about 2 tablespoons for garnish. Stir the remainder into the pastry cream.

Stuff the apples with the pastry cream using a small spoon or a filled pastry bag, allowing some of the pudding to mound on top of each apple. Sprinkle with reserved currants and pine nuts. Chill until ready to serve.

Desserts and Sweet Snacks

Puddings and Gelatins

Italian Pastry Cream

One of the foundations of Italian dessert making, this is basically the best pudding you'll ever taste. Very notably, it becomes the luscious base for fresh fruits in a fruit crostata.

Makes about 2¼ cups

3 egg yolks

½ cup plus 2 tablespoons confectioner's sugar

5 tablespoons unbleached all-purpose flour

2 cups milk

¼ teaspoon vanilla extract

Grated zest of 1 lemon

Place the egg yolks and sugar in a heavy saucepan. Off the heat, beat until the mixture turns pale yellow and foamy. Gradually beat in the flour, a little at a time.

In another saucepan, heat the milk over medium-low heat just until small bubbles form around the edges. Slowly add hot milk to egg mixture, stirring constantly.

Place the pan over a larger pan of boiling water or in a double-boiler and cook for about 5 minutes, whisking constantly with a wire whisk. The pastry cream is ready when it coats the back of a wooden spoon. Do not let the mixture come to a boil. Remove from the heat and keep whisking a few minutes until the bottom of the pan cools off. Stir in the vanilla and grated lemon zest.

Transfer to a bowl. Let cool. Cover and chill until needed. It keeps, refrigerated, for several days.

Rum Custard

When my mother was growing up in Italy, rum babas were often taken as gifts when visiting a sick friend or relative. Considered restorative, they served to lift the spirits and offer nourishment. This simple rum custard strikes a similar, but more restrained, note.

Makes 6 servings

Unsalted butter for custard cups

4 eggs

½ cup sugar

2 cups milk

Tiny pinch salt

2 tablespoons dark rum

Preheat the oven to 325°F. Butter six ½-cup custard cups.

In a bowl, lightly beat the eggs. Add the sugar, milk, salt, and rum, and whisk together. Strain the liquid into the prepared cups.

Place the cups in the oven in a shallow pan partly filled with very hot water. (A large sauté pan with an ovenproof handle works well. Heat the water on the stove, then place the sauté pan in the oven.) Bake custards for 40 minutes, or until just firm. Remove from pan and let cool. Serve at warm room temperature or lightly chilled.

Perfumed Panna Cotta

I've infused this exquisite dessert, a simple composition of cream, milk, sugar, and gelatin, with the essence of bitter almonds and orange flower water.

To achieve the flavor of bitter almonds, unavailable here, turn to convenient almond extract, which derives its flavor from the highly aromatic nut.

Please do not garnish the panna cotta. This means no fruits or sauces of any kind, as they would detract from its creamy white purity and subtle flavor and fragrance. **Makes 6 servings**

1 envelope unflavored gelatin

2 cups milk

1 cup fresh, pure heavy cream, without preservatives or density enhancers

¼ cup sugar

1 teaspoon almond extract (see headnote)

1 teaspoon orange blossom water

In a saucepan, sprinkle the gelatin evenly over ½ cup of the milk and let stand 5 minutes to soften. Over low heat, stir well until the gelatin dissolves completely, about 5 minutes. Stir in the remaining milk, cream, and sugar, and cook until small bubbles form around the edges of the pan.

Remove from the heat. Stir in the almond extract and orange blossom water. Let cool a little. Pour into 6 small ½-cup stemmed ice cream dishes or ½-cup custard cups. Refrigerate, covered with a sheet of wax paper, until firm. Serve cold or cool.

Watermelon "Pudding"   Here is a recipe for

gelo di melone, the exotic pudding I first tasted in Palermo, Sicily, at the

tender age of twelve.

Select a very deeply colored and sugary-sweet watermelon. Serve

small portions since this pudding has an Arabian nights sweetness to it. For

a special evocation of place, garnish the dessert with jasmine blossoms.

See page 89 for a recipe for Watermelon Ice that uses the same fas-

cinating medley of ingredients.   **Makes 4 to 5 servings**

2½ pounds ripe watermelon

¼ cup sugar

¼ cup cornstarch

1 teaspoon orange blossom water

Pinch ground cinnamon

1½ ounces bittersweet chocolate, cut into small pieces

2 tablespoons chopped pistachios plus extra for sprinkling

Cut the watermelon into chunks and remove the rind and seeds. Put watermelon through a
food mill or process in a blender to get about 2 cups juice.

Combine the watermelon juice, sugar, and cornstarch in a saucepan, and stir until the cornstarch completely dissolves. Bring the mixture to a boil over high heat, stirring constantly. Let

boil for a few minutes until the mixture is bright red. Stir in the orange blossom water and cinnamon.

Pour into 4 or 5 small ice cream goblets. When cool, stir in chocolate pieces and pistachios.

Refrigerate until well chilled. To serve, sprinkle with chopped pistachios and, if available, garnish with jasmine flowers.

Gelatina di Espresso

Good gelatin desserts shimmer and wobble. They appear solid, but melt under the tongue in a moment.

A little gelatin added to freshly brewed espresso turns this dark aromatic liquid into just barely solid form. Sugar the coffee sparingly so that it maintains its slightly bitter edge, and serve the gelatina in small stemmed goblets with a cloud of pure whipped cream atop it.

Espresso gelatin makes for a summertime offering that is both cooling dessert and revivifying coffee. It also is a great afternoon pick-me-up.

Makes 4 servings

1 tablespoon (1 envelope) unflavored gelatin

2 tablespoons cold water

2 cups freshly brewed espresso, sugared to taste

Heavy cream, whipped, with or without a touch of sugar

In a bowl, sprinkle the gelatin over the cold water and let sit for about 5 minutes. Add the hot sweetened espresso and stir until the gelatin melts completely.

Pour the mixture into 4 small ½-cup dessert goblets. Refrigerate until firm.

Just before serving, top with a big dollop of whipped cream.

Cakes, Crostatas, and Cookies

Chocolate and Espresso Cake

Espresso refers to one of the flavorings in this cake and also to the speed and ease of its preparation. In the Italian tradition, this is a single-layer cake of modest height; no frosting is required. The flavor of the espresso becomes more intense the day after baking.

Almonds and walnuts, very finely ground, are used in place of flour. A hand-cranked nut grinder or cheese grater produces the best results——fine, powdery flakes of almonds and walnuts. But an electric coffee grinder works well, too. Just grind nuts in small batches with a bit of the sugar to prevent nuts from forming a paste. **Makes 6 to 8 servings**

¾ cup whole unpeeled almonds

½ cup chopped walnuts

4 ounces bittersweet chocolate

5 eggs, separated

¾ cup sugar

2 tablespoons very finely ground espresso

Unsalted butter and flour for cake pan

Finely grind the nuts using either a hand-cranked nut grinder, coffee grinder, or blender.

Melt the chocolate in the upper half of a double boiler.

continued

47

In a mixing bowl, using a fork, lightly beat the egg yolks. Stir in the sugar, nuts, melted chocolate, and espresso. Mix well.

Preheat the oven to 350°F. Butter and lightly flour a round 9-inch springform pan.

In another mixing bowl, beat the egg whites until stiff peaks form. Carefully fold the egg whites into the chocolate mixture. Pour into the prepared cake pan.

Place in the oven and bake for about 55 minutes. It is ready when a thin skewer inserted in the center comes out clean. Remove from the oven and let rest a few minutes, unmold, and serve.

Sweet Spaghettini Torta

Pasta lovers will find this torta irresistible. Swirls of spaghettini strands are bound together with creamy ricotta. Without adding the rum, the torta is great for children, served as a dessert or an afternoon snack. Adults will find that the rum adds a subtle note of sophistication. This wholesome cake is ideal picnic fare, since it's easy to eat out of hand. **Makes 6 to 8 servings**

½ pound spaghettini

2 cups ricotta

4 eggs, beaten

¾ cup sugar

½ cup chopped almonds

Grated zest of 1 orange

Unsalted butter for baking dish

¼ cup unflavored bread crumbs

3 tablespoons dark rum, optional

Bring a large pot of water to a boil over high heat. Add the spaghettini and cook until al dente.

Preheat the oven to 375°F.

Meanwhile, in a bowl, combine the ricotta, eggs, sugar, almonds, and orange zest, and blend until creamy.

continued

Drain the spaghettini and transfer to a bowl. Add the ricotta mixture, stirring it in a little at a time until it is evenly distributed.

Butter an oval baking dish that is about 2 inches deep. Reserve 1 tablespoon of bread crumbs. Use the remaining crumbs to coat the inside of the baking dish, tilting the dish back and forth to coat the inside evenly. Turn the dish upside down and tap it to shake out any excess.

Pour the ricotta-spaghettini mixture into the prepared baking dish and top with the reserved bread crumbs. Bake for 50 to 60 minutes, or until a thin wooden skewer inserted in the center comes out clean. Let cool to room temperature and unmold. If using the rum, use a toothpick to prick about 20 little holes into the top of the cake. Carefully spoon the rum over the top of the cake, spooning a little at a time and letting it seep in before adding more. Let rest for at least 1 hour to let the flavors mellow.

If serving the same day, there is no need to refrigerate the cake. Otherwise, refrigerate it for up to several days. Bring the cake back to room temperature before serving.

Italian Rice Cake   When I first began my exploration of Italian food, one of my earliest attempts at dessert was a rice cake. It was love at first bite. The creamy sweetness of the rice cooked in milk, the way the rice became imbued with flavor, its dense and moist texture—all added up to one of the best desserts I'd ever eaten. And I still feel that way today.

There are many versions of rice cake. The one offered here is chock-ablock with pistachios, pine nuts, walnuts, lemon zest, and candied orange rind. Purchase unsalted, roasted pistachios.

A great feature of rice cake is that it keeps well. In fact, it's best when made a day in advance to allow the flavors to mellow. To store the cake, wrap it tightly in waxed paper or aluminum foil and refrigerate.

Makes 6 to 8 servings

3 cups milk

¾ cup rice, preferably Italian arborio

4 eggs, beaten

½ cup sugar

¼ cup shelled, peeled, and chopped pistachios (see Note)

¼ cup chopped walnuts

¼ cup pine nuts, lightly toasted (see Note)

Scant ¼ cup finely diced candied orange peel (page 113)

¼ teaspoon vanilla

2 tablespoons unsalted butter, softened to room temperature

Grated zest of ½ lemon

Unsalted butter and flour for cake pan

Powdered sugar

In a saucepan over medium heat, bring the milk to the brink of a boil. Add the rice and stir. Reduce the heat to low. Cover and cook the rice at a gentle simmer, stirring often to prevent sticking. The rice is ready when it becomes very soft and the mixture is creamy, about 30 minutes. Remove the pan from the heat and let cool.

Preheat the oven to 350°F.

Stir the eggs into the rice, then add the remaining ingredients except the butter, flour, and powdered sugar.

Butter and flour a 10-inch round cake pan. Add the rice mixture.

Place the pan in the oven and bake for 1 hour, or until the cake is firm and a thin skewer inserted in the center comes out clean. Remove from the oven and cool to lukewarm. Unmold the cake. Before serving, dust with powdered sugar.

Note: To toast the pine nuts, spread on a baking sheet and toast in a 350°F oven for about 10 minutes. Let cool. To peel pistachios, wrap the nuts in a dish towel and rub vigorously. Don't worry if some peel remains.

Semolina Cake

In this cross between a pudding and a cake, fine semolina becomes transformed into a light, creamy dessert studded with tender candied orange peel and pistachios and just a hint of rum flavor. **Makes 8 servings**

½ cup finely diced candied orange peel (page 113)

4 tablespoons rum

2 tablespoons unsalted butter

A little semolina to sprinkle in pan

4 cups milk

Small pinch salt

⅔ cup semolina

1⅓ cups sugar

½ cup unsalted, shelled pistachios, peeled and coarsely chopped (see Note)

4 eggs, lightly beaten

Place the candied orange peel in a small bowl and add rum. Set aside.

Preheat the oven to 375°F. Butter a 6-inch soufflé dish. Sprinkle with semolina and shake out excess. Set aside.

Place the milk and salt in a saucepan, and bring to the brink of a boil over low heat. Add the semolina in a thin stream, whisking continuously with a wire whisk. Continue stirring until the semolina thickens and begins to pull away from the sides of the pan. Remove from the heat and continue stirring for 1 to 2 minutes. Stir in the sugar. Add the candied orange peel and rum mixture and the pistachios, and stir until evenly distributed. Quickly stir in the beaten eggs.

Pour into the prepared dish. Bake for 1 hour, or until firm. Remove from the oven and cool to room temperature. Refrigerate to firm up pudding, about 30 minutes. Unmold. Serve cool or at room temperature.

Note: To peel pistachios, wrap the nuts in a dish towel and rub vigorously. Don't worry if some peel remains.

Carrot and Almond Cake
Set aside any preconceived notions about carrot cake. This rather elegant version uses finely ground almonds and crushed amaretti cookies in place of flour. Typical of Italian cakes, it is a single layer, with just a dusting of powdered sugar on top and no cream cheese in sight.

Restrained, yes. But seductively good. **Makes 6 to 8 servings**

2 cups whole unpeeled almonds

½ cup crushed amaretti cookies

2 teaspoons baking powder

4 eggs, separated

¼ cup sugar

Grated zest of 1 lemon

A few drops almond extract

2½ cups carrots (about 5 medium), peeled and coarsely grated

Unsalted butter and flour for pan

Preheat the oven to 350°F.

Grind the almonds in a nut grinder, coffee grinder, or blender. In a mixing bowl, stir together the ground almonds, amaretti, and baking powder.

In another mixing bowl, beat the egg yolks with sugar until pale yellow and creamy. Stir in the lemon zest and almond extract. Add to the almond mixture along with the grated carrots.

Butter and flour a 9-inch springform pan.

In a clean mixing bowl, beat the egg whites until stiff and gently fold into egg-yolk mixture. Pour into the prepared pan.

Place the pan in the preheated oven and bake for 50 to 60 minutes, or until a skewer inserted in the center comes out clean. Remove from the oven and let cool to room temperature. Release the sides of the pan and transfer to a cake dish. Serve at room temperature. When completely cool, wrap in aluminum foil and store at room temperature. This cake keeps well for days.

Ricotta Soufflé

Don't be intimidated by the word *soufflé*. All you do here is fold fluffy beaten egg whites into sweetened ricotta and, magically, the cake rises and swells like a soufflé. Served straight from the oven, the cake is elegant and light as a feather, each bite melting onto the tongue. As it cools, it deflates and becomes dense and moist, and slightly more rustic in texture. I can't decide which way I like it better since both are delectable. **Makes 4 to 6 servings**

Unsalted butter for soufflé dish

3 pairs (6 individual) amaretti cookies, crushed

12 ounces ricotta

½ cup sugar

½ cup ground peeled almonds (see Note)

Grated zest of 1 lemon

5 egg whites

Preheat the oven to 350°F. Butter a 6-inch soufflé dish and line with amaretti crumbs.

In a bowl, combine the ricotta, sugar, almonds, and lemon zest. Stir until creamy and well incorporated.

In another bowl, beat the egg whites until firm. With a spatula, carefully fold the ricotta mixture into the egg whites a little at a time.

Pour the mixture into the prepared dish. Bake for about 35 minutes, or until a wooden skewer inserted in the center comes out clean. Serve immediately or at room temperature.

Note: Grind the almonds in a nut grinder, coffee grinder, or blender.

Tender Fruit and Rum Cake

Unsulfured golden sultana raisins, plump apricots, moist medjool dates, and black figs, infused with the flavor of rum and a tender golden crumb, make this the lightest and most delicate of fruit cakes.

You may have to go to a natural foods store for high-quality dried fruits, but it is worth the effort. I find it easier to dice sticky dried fruits by cutting them with scissors. **Makes 6 to 8 servings**

½ cup diced pitted medjool dates

½ cup diced dried black figs

½ cup diced dried apricots

½ cup unsulfured sultana raisins

½ cup dark rum

Unsalted butter and flour for cake pan

1¾ cups unbleached all-purpose flour

2 teaspoons baking powder

½ cup (1 stick) unsalted butter

1 cup sugar

2 eggs, lightly beaten

⅔ cup milk

1 teaspoon vanilla

Place the fruits and rum in a bowl, and let rest for several hours, stirring every so often.

Preheat the oven to 350°F. Butter and flour a 10-inch cake pan.

In a bowl, combine the flour and baking powder. In another bowl, cream the butter until soft. Gradually add the sugar to the butter and beat until creamy. Add the beaten eggs, a little at a time. Carefully beat in the flour and milk, alternating them, beginning and ending with flour. Add the vanilla and stir. The batter will be thick. Drain the fruits of any excess rum. Stir the fruits into batter. Transfer the batter to the prepared pan.

Bake for about 35 minutes, or until a wooden skewer inserted in the center comes out clean. Let cool in the pan. This cake lasts for days unrefrigerated, wrapped in waxed paper or foil.

Sweet Olive Oil Quick Bread

Extra-virgin olive oil is the secret ingredient in this moist, dense, lightly sweet cake.

Perfect as an afternoon snack or for breakfast with a cup of fluffy cappuccino.

Makes 8 servings

2½ cups unbleached all-purpose flour

2 teaspoons baking powder

Pinch salt

1 cup sugar

2 eggs, lightly beaten

¾ cup milk

½ cup extra-virgin olive oil

½ cup unsulfured sultana raisins

Grated zest of 1 lemon

Unsalted butter for loaf pan

¼ cup pine nuts

Preheat oven to 350°F.

In a mixing bowl, stir together the flour, baking powder, and salt. Stir in the sugar. Add the eggs, milk, and olive oil, and beat well.

Toss the raisins in a little flour to coat them lightly. Add the raisins and lemon zest to the flour and egg mixture and stir to distribute evenly.

Butter and flour a loaf pan. Transfer the batter into the pan and smooth the surface. Sprinkle the top with pine nuts. Bake for 55 minutes, or until a thin skewer inserted in the center comes out dry. Let cool for a few minutes. Unmold and cool on a rack.

Cantaloupe Crostata

I was nineteen when I first saw and tasted a European-style fruit tart. I was in Rome, dining at the home of relatives. When the crostata was brought out, I'd never seen such a dazzlingly pretty dessert. The fresh fruits and pastry cream atop a crisp sugary crust more than lived up to their appearance. I can still see the light playing on those colored fruits.

The second most memorable fruit tart I tasted was on a trip to Puglia, at the very bottom of the heel of the boot. It was a balmy summer night on the terrace of a *ristorante* facing the sea with an elegant collection of Italians dressed in ultimate summer chic. After a meal featuring brilliantly fresh seafood, I was served a crostata topped with sweet melon slices.

Here's my version. The crust is crisp, the pastry cream highly perfumed with lemon, and the melon of choice is cantaloupe——for its dense flesh, beautiful peach color, and intense perfume. And no glaze, no apricot preserves or anything else to interfere with the freshness and purity of the fruit. **Makes 6 to 8 servings**

continued

1 recipe Italian Pastry Crust (recipe follows)

1 recipe Italian Pastry Cream (page 36)

Slices of ripe but firm cantaloupe

Prepare and bake pastry crust according to recipe. When the crust is cool, fill with pastry cream, spreading it evenly. Top with melon slices and serve.

If preparing the crostata in advance, the baked crust can be filled with the pastry cream in the morning and refrigerated until evening. Top with fruit just before serving.

Italian Pastry Crust A sugary crust for fruit and pastry cream tarts. This dough comes together effortlessly, so proceed without fear. Makes 1 crust plus extra for a few cookies or a couple of turnovers

1³⁄₄ cups unbleached all-purpose flour

¹⁄₂ cup sugar

Tiny pinch salt

¹⁄₂ cup (1 stick) unsalted butter, cut up

1 egg, lightly beaten

1 egg yolk

In a bowl, stir together the flour, sugar, and salt. Add the butter, egg, and egg yolk, and mix with a wooden spoon. Then use your fingertips to bring the mixture together. Transfer to a work surface. Knead quickly, using the heel of your hand, just until the mixture forms a smooth ball.

Alternatively, you can use a food processor to make the dough. First cream together the butter and sugar. Then add the flour, eggs, and salt. Stop mixing when the mixture begins to form a ball. Knead briefly to form a smooth ball.

Wrap the dough tightly. Chill for at least 30 minutes. (Yes, this dough can be frozen.)

To bake the crust, preheat the oven to 350°F.

Butter and flour a 9-inch tart pan. Roll out the dough to a diameter that is roughly 2 inches larger than the pan. Line the pan with the dough. Allow a generous amount of dough on the sides of the pan, since the pastry will shrink when cooked. Prick the surface of the dough with a fork.

Bake for 10 to 15 minutes, or until golden. Let cool.

Aunt Ida's Famous Cookies

Chock-full of chopped dark chocolate and almonds, these wonderful meringue cookies are chewy and crunchy and melt in your mouth all at the same time. It's hard to stop eating them. The memory of Aunt Ida lives on in what may be the best chocolate chip cookies you've ever eaten! **Makes about 45 cookies**

3 egg whites

1 tablespoon white vinegar

¼ teaspoon salt

1 cup sugar

1 teaspoon vanilla extract

½ pound coarsely ground or chopped toasted almonds (see Note)

½ pound coarsely ground or chopped bittersweet chocolate

Preheat the oven to 250°F.

Beat the egg whites with the vinegar and salt until stiff but not dry. Very gradually add the sugar and continue to beat until meringue forms stiff peaks. Gently fold in the vanilla, almonds, and chocolate.

Line 3 or 4 baking sheets with parchment paper or aluminum foil. Drop the mixture by teaspoonfuls about 1 inch apart on the prepared cookie sheets. Place in the oven and bake until firm, about 45 minutes. Let cookies cool on the cookie sheet. Store in a tin or airtight glass jar.

Note: To toast the nuts, spread on a baking sheet and toast at 350°F for 10 minutes. Let cool. Grind the nuts in a nut grinder, blender, or food processor with a few tablespoons of sugar from the recipe, or chop by hand.

Ladyfingers

Ladyfingers In Italy ladyfingers, *savoiardi*, were being made as far back as the seventeenth century. To this day, they are an essential element in many Italian desserts.

Homemade ladyfingers are easy to make, and are a world apart from the commercial kind: more tender, less friable, and not too sweet. They are perfect cookies for children.

A little grated orange zest would make a nice addition.

Makes about 24 cookies

Unsalted butter and flour for baking sheets
½ cup unbleached all-purpose flour
¼ cup potato starch (see Note)
Pinch salt
4 eggs, warmed to room temperature and separated
½ cup sugar
1 teaspoon vanilla extract
Powdered sugar

Preheat the oven to 400°F.

Butter and lightly flour 2 baking sheets. In a bowl, stir together the flour, potato starch, and salt.

continued

In another bowl, beat together the egg yolks and 2 tablespoons of the sugar until they are pale yellow, thick, and creamy. Stir in the vanilla.

In another bowl, beat the egg whites until foamy, then gradually beat in the remaining sugar until the whites are stiff and form peaks.

Gently fold ¼ of the egg yolk mixture into the beaten egg whites. Then gradually fold the flour and remaining egg whites into the egg yolk mixture, alternating them. The batter should be light and fluffy.

Spoon the batter into a pastry bag in which you have inserted a ½-inch plain tip. Pipe 4-inch-long strips of batter about 1 inch apart on the prepared baking sheets. Sift a generous amount of powdered sugar over the tops of the cookies.

Bake for about 8 to 10 minutes, or until cookies are golden. Transfer to a cooling rack. Ladyfingers keep well in an airtight container for several weeks.

Note: Potato starch can be found in the kosher or imported foods section of supermarkets.

Hazelnut and Lemon Meringues

Brittle, sugary meringue cookies, accompanied by a tiny cup of fragrant dark espresso, make a wonderful afternoon pick-me-up. This Sicilian version is flavored with toasted hazelnuts and fresh aromatic lemon peel.

You can make these cookies using the egg whites left over after making pastry cream or ice cream. **Makes about 30 cookies**

2 egg whites

Pinch salt

6 tablespoons sugar

1 cup chopped, toasted hazelnuts (see Note)

Zest of $\frac{1}{2}$ lemon, preferably organic

Whip the egg whites with salt until they turn white and form soft peaks. Very slowly add the sugar. Whip until the meringue is firm. Gently fold in the hazelnuts and lemon zest.

Line 2 baking sheets with parchment paper or aluminum foil. Drop the meringue by teaspoonfuls about 1 inch apart on the prepared cookie sheets. Bake at 275°F for 50 to 55 minutes, or until cookies are firm and lightly colored.

Let cool on the cookie sheet. Store in a tin or airtight glass jar.

Note: To toast hazelnuts, spread unpeeled nuts on a baking sheet and toast at 350°F for 10 minutes. Let cool. Wrap them in a dish towel and rub vigorously to remove loose peels. Chop finely.

Ice Cream,
Ice Cream
Fantasies, and
an Ice

Pink Honeydew Ice Cream

I call it pink honeydew, although technically, it is orange-fleshed, and it is one of my favorite melons. Here, it is given just enough richness to qualify as ice cream but not so much as to interfere with the flavor of the melon. **Makes 1 quart**

¾ pound diced orange-fleshed honeydew

½ cup sugar

¾ cup cream

In a blender, puree the honeydew and sugar until liquefied.

In a bowl, beat the cream until soft and slightly thickened but not stiff.

In a bowl, combine the fruit puree and whipped cream and stir. Refrigerate until the mixture is very cold.

Process according to the ice cream maker manufacturer's directions. The ice cream is ready to eat immediately or freeze for several hours to firm it up. To store, transfer ice cream to a plastic container with a tight-fitting lid and place in the freezer. Place in refrigerator 20 minutes before serving to soften the texture slightly.

Orange Blossom Ice Cream

Exquisite is the word for this ice cream, infused with the essence of orange blossoms and studded with almonds and pistachios. **Makes 1½ quarts**

2 cups milk

1 cup heavy cream

4 large egg yolks

¾ cup sugar

2 tablespoons orange blossom water

½ teaspoon vanilla extract

⅓ cup toasted, peeled almonds, cut in half crosswise (see Note)

¼ cup peeled unsalted pistachios, cut in half crosswise (see Note)

In a heavy-bottomed medium saucepan over medium heat, heat the milk and cream until small bubbles form around the edge of the pan. Remove from the heat.

In a large bowl, stir together the egg yolks and sugar until foamy. Slowly stir in the hot milk and cream mixture. Return to the saucepan. Cook mixture over low heat until it thickens slightly, a matter of a few minutes. It should very lightly coat the back of a wooden spoon. Let cool.

Stir in the orange blossom water and vanilla extract. Pour into the ice cream maker and process according to the manufacturer's directions. When the ice cream is at the desired consistency, stir in the nuts. Transfer to a plastic container and freeze for several hours until firm.

Note: To toast the nuts, spread them on a baking sheet and toast in a 350°F oven for about 10 minutes. To peel the pistachios, wrap them in a dish towel and rub vigorously. Don't worry if some peel remains.

Rum Ice Cream

Rum Ice Cream This creamy, cooling rum ice cream is infused with the flavors of orange and lemon peel. It is delectable served with fruits such as whole peeled fresh figs. **Makes 4 to 6 servings**

2½ cups milk

½ cup heavy cream

Peel of ½ fresh lemon, yellow part only, removed in long strips with a vegetable peeler

Peel of ½ fresh orange, orange part only, removed in long strips with a vegetable peeler

4 egg yolks

¾ cup sugar

2 tablespoons dark rum

In a heavy saucepan over medium heat, slowly heat the milk, cream, and citrus peels until small bubbles form around the edge of the pan. Remove from heat and let cool briefly.

In a bowl, beat together the egg yolks and sugar until pale yellow and creamy. Through a strainer, slowly add hot milk to the egg mixture, stirring often. Add rum and stir.

Return the mixture to the saucepan. Stirring constantly, cook over medium heat until the mixture thickens slightly, a few minutes. It should lightly coat the back of a wooden spoon. Do not let it come to a boil. Let cool. Refrigerate until well chilled.

Pour into the ice cream maker and process according to the manufacturer's directions. Transfer to a plastic container and freeze until firm.

Open-Face Ice Cream Sandwich

The combination of bread and ice cream may sound strange, but it is a time-honored custom in Italy. In *Panini, Bruschetta, Crostini*, I suggest filling a brioche with ice cream. Here, vanilla ice cream is spread on a slice of bread that has been glossed with tangy lemon marmalade. **Makes 1 serving**

Lemon marmalade

1 slice firm crusty bread

Vanilla ice cream

Spread marmalade thinly on bread, making sure to include bits of peel. Then spread ice cream generously over the marmalade. Eat immediately.

Coppa Barocca In Italy during the summer, chairs and tables spill out of caffès onto the sidewalks, where people sit four and five rows deep, enjoying the passing parade and cooling off with an enticing drink or a scoop or two of ice cream.

Some caffès offer baroque concoctions of fruits, ice cream, and liqueurs in oversized goblets that are nearly impossible to resist. And why resist? It's so much better to give in to temptation and while away some time, leisurely slipping your silvery spoon into the goblet's colorful and lush depths.

The following recipe combines rum ice cream and summer fruit for a taste of Italian caffè life. **Makes 1 serving**

2 scoops **Rum Ice Cream** (page 79)

2 finely diced ripe apricots or other summer fruit, lightly sweetened
(about 1 teaspoon per apricot)

5 peeled raw almonds, split

1 heaping teaspoon candied orange peel (page 113), finely diced

Scoop the ice cream into a chilled dessert goblet. Spoon diced apricots and any juices that have formed over the top. Sprinkle with almond halves and candied orange peel.

Strawberries Villa Borghese

This is an ice cream fantasy I enjoyed one gorgeous spring day at a caffè on the edge of Villa Borghese, the sprawling public park high up on a belvedere overlooking the historic center of Rome.

In this recipe, a discreet scoop of vanilla ice cream is topped with strawberries and a generous cloud of whipped cream. It's the contrast of the dense, cold ice cream and the light-as-air whipped cream that makes this memorable. **Makes 2 servings**

¼ cup heavy cream

2 small scoops vanilla ice cream

½ cup small ripe, red strawberries, sliced

In a bowl, whip the cream until thick. Place 1 scoop of ice cream in each of 2 goblets. Spoon strawberries over ice cream. Top with a large dollop of whipped cream. Serve immediately.

Whipped Cream–Filled Brioche

Although not an ice cream dessert, in Italy this sweet snack is traditionally offered in caffè/bars and *gelaterie*. While it feels like an indulgence, it is basically composed of a small amount of cream, whipped to an airy lightness, and a tender, wholesome brioche.

Cream that contains stabilizers to extend its shelf life or density enhancers loses its sweet, fresh flavor. Look for heavy cream without additives in natural food stores and high-quality markets. **Makes 4 servings**

½ cup heavy cream

1 to 2 teaspoons sugar

4 brioches, purchased freshly made from a good bakery

In a bowl, whip the cream until thick. Beat in the sugar. Split the brioches lengthwise, not cutting all the way through, and fill with whipped cream. A little messy to eat, but very good.

Mediterranean Surprise

In all my cookbooks I've included a recipe from *A Snob in the Kitchen*, written by legendary Italian fashion designer Simonetta. Her recipes are stylish and sophisticated, but always tempered by an Italian earthiness and simplicity. This ice cream dessert is a Simonetta recipe that, in fashion terms, is a bit more haute couture.

Culinarily speaking, a dish with "surprise" in the title generally means that it contains a concealed or unexpected ingredient. Here, the surprise is ice cream concealed by a delicately browned meringue.

Make sure that the ice cream is frozen rock-solid before topping it with meringue and sending it into the oven. **Makes 6 servings**

1 large ripe pineapple
1 quart vanilla ice cream
4 egg whites
¼ cup sugar

Halve the pineapple lengthwise. With a knife, cut away the flesh, leaving a hollow in each half. Discard the core of the pineapple and cut the flesh into small pieces. Drain off any excess juices.

Let the ice cream soften a bit. Then blend in the pineapple. Quickly pack the mixture into the shells leaving a border of pineapple shell exposed. Wrap in plastic and freeze until very hard, several hours or, better yet, overnight.

Whip the egg whites until firm, gradually beating in sugar.

Preheat the oven to 450°F. Remove the pineapple shells from the freezer and spoon the meringue on top, completely covering the ice cream. Place in the oven for 3 to 4 minutes, or until the meringue is firm and lightly browned.

To serve, cut through the meringue, ice cream, and pineapple to make layered slices. Serve immediately.

Date Shake During my childhood in southern California, my family and I would sometimes go for a drive to Indio, a small desert town near Palm Springs. Date palms flourished there in the midst of miles and miles of sand.

We would always stop at a stand that sold date shakes——a rich, creamy blend of ice cream and dates. I can still see the little stand, bathed in the clear desert light——the straggly rose garden in front with the most fragrant red roses imaginable, the scent of parched grass, and high above our heads, huge clusters of rusty-orange dates dangling from the tops of fringed dusty palms.

For this exotic shake I prefer to use medjool dates with their dark gold, moist flesh and honeyed flavor. But fresh deglet dates can also be used; just double the quantity. **Makes 1 shake**

8 plump dates, preferably medjool, peeled and pitted

1 cup milk plus a little extra if needed to thin shake

2 scoops (about 1 cup) vanilla ice cream

Coarsely chop the dates. Place dates in a blender. Add 1 cup milk and blend until smooth. Add ice cream and blend for a few seconds until thick and creamy. Blend in a little more milk if shake is too thick to pour. Pour into a tall glass and serve.

Watermelon Ice   This is an icy cold, highly refreshing version of *gelo di melone*, a Sicilian watermelon "pudding" (see page 40). You have to taste the combination of bittersweet chocolate, orange blossom water, green pistachios, and darkest pink, almost red, watermelon juice to appreciate its flavor and exotic appearance. A little *trompe l'oeil*: the small squares of cut-up chocolate look like watermelon seeds. Use only very sweet and deeply colored watermelon flesh.   **Makes 5 to 6 servings**

3 pounds ripe watermelon

½ cup sugar

2 teaspoons orange blossom water

2 tablespoons dark chocolate, cut into small pieces about the size of watermelon seeds

2 tablespoons unsalted pistachios, peeled and lightly toasted (see Note)

Cinnamon

Cut the rind off the watermelon. You should have approximately 2 pounds of flesh. Pick out the seeds. Cut watermelon into chunks and put through a food mill or food processor until reduced to a liquid. In a bowl, stir the sugar into the watermelon liquid and let rest a few minutes until sugar melts. Stir in the orange blossom water. Freeze the mixture in an ice cream maker, according to manufacturer's directions. Stir in the chocolate and pistachios. Store in the freezer in a plastic container.

continued

Remove from freezer and spoon into chilled goblets. Serve sprinkled with a light dusting of cinnamon.

Note: To peel pistachios, wrap nuts in a dish towel and rub them vigorously. Don't worry if some peel remains. To toast the nuts, spread on a baking sheet and toast in a 350°F oven for about 10 minutes.

Watermelon

Sweet Fresh Cheeses and a Savory Cheese Dessert

Ricotta with Cocoa and Brandy

Not too rich but wonderfully creamy-tasting, ricotta requires just minimal flavoring to become the best of desserts. Here, I call for Dutch-process cocoa, with its dark color and pronounced bittersweet taste. Add a little brandy for a kick, toasted nuts for crunch, and that's all you need.

This simple dessert can be prepared up to a day in advance or eaten immediately. Served in small portions, it makes an elegant ending to a meal, or enjoy it as a sweet snack. **Makes 4 to 6 servings**

1 pound whole milk ricotta

¼ cup sugar

3 tablespoons dark cocoa plus extra for sifting over top

3 tablespoons brandy

¼ cup unpeeled almonds, toasted and coarsely chopped (see Note)

Powdered sugar

To remove the lumps in the ricotta, use a spatula to push it through a fine-mesh sieve, repeating the process a second time if desired. Alternatively, whirl the ricotta in a blender or food processor until smooth.

In a bowl, combine the ricotta with the sugar, cocoa, and brandy, and stir well to combine. Refrigerate until needed.

continued

To serve, spoon the mixture into small ice cream goblets (I like the little metal ones available in restaurant supply stores) or small soufflé cups. Dust with cocoa powder, sprinkle the top with toasted almonds, then dust with powdered sugar.

Note: To toast the nuts, spread on a baking sheet and toast in a 350°F oven for about 10 minutes.

Ricotta with Honey and Almonds

This little mountain of ricotta drizzled with golden honey and topped with toasted almonds is one of the easiest desserts to prepare as well as being one of the most beautiful. It makes a satisfying and nutritious afternoon snack. It can also be served at breakfast. **Makes 4 to 6 servings**

1 pound whole milk ricotta

2 tablespoons honey

¼ cup coarsely chopped, freshly toasted almonds (see Note)

If the ricotta is moist, drain it in a colander lined with cheesecloth for several hours. Transfer the ricotta onto a serving platter and shape into a mound. Drizzle with honey and sprinkle with toasted almonds.

Note: To toast the nuts, spread on a baking sheet and toast in a 350°F oven for about 10 minutes. Let cool.

Fresh Figs with Goat Cheese and Mint

Here, a spoonful of fresh goat cheese mixed with walnuts and mint is the filling for sweet ripe figs. The final touch is a gilding of musky-sweet honey. **Makes 4 servings**

½ cup (4 ounces) fresh goat cheese

2 tablespoons finely chopped walnuts, plus extra for garnish

1 tablespoon finely chopped mint leaves

8 ripe figs

Honey for drizzling

In a small bowl, mix together the goat cheese, walnuts, and mint.

Cut the stems off the figs. Make 2 vertical cuts in the form of a cross in each fig, without cutting all the way through. Gently open up the sections to create a cavity in the center of the fig.

Gently place a heaping teaspoon of filling in the center of each fig. Carefully re-form the fruit by pressing the fig sections into the cheese.

Place on a platter and refrigerate until ready to serve. Remove figs from the refrigerator about 15 minutes before serving. Figs should be at cool room temperature. Drizzle with honey and lightly dust with finely chopped walnuts.

Pears with Mascarpone

A topping of creamy mascarpone complements the subtle flavor of the pear without overwhelming it. Sprinkled with sugar and dusted with cocoa, the pear becomes a simple and elegant ending to a meal.

Make sure the pear is fully ripe. A perfectly ripe pear is juicy with a slight crispness to the flesh. Pears ripen from the inside out, so don't wait until the pear is soft on the outside, since by then the flesh will be mealy. If the pear yields to gentle pressure near the stem end, and has a fragrant aroma, it is ripe. **Makes 2 servings**

1 pear

½ lemon

3 heaping tablespoons mascarpone

1 teaspoon sugar or more

European-style Dutch-process cocoa, to lightly dust the pear

Peel the pear. Cut in half lengthwise and remove the core. Slice a little off the bottom of each pear half to stabilize it. Rub the pear halves with lemon juice to prevent darkening of the flesh.

Spread the mascarpone evenly over the top of the pear halves, smoothing to cover cut sides completely. Sprinkle with sugar and dust lightly with cocoa. If making in advance, spread the pears with the mascarpone and cover well. Refrigerate. Remove from refrigerator 20 minutes before serving. Just before serving, sprinkle with sugar and dust with cocoa.

Dates Filled with Sweetened Ricotta

Here, medjool dates are pitted and filled with sweetened ricotta flavored with finely chopped almonds and lemon rind. You can also add a bit of orange blossom water to the ricotta mixture to add to its exotic, desert-oasis appeal.

I adore the creamy, honeyed flesh of dates, especially medjool dates, large, dark, and fleshy. These are available in the produce section of many natural foods stores.

Serve the dates as dessert or as a nourishing snack.

Makes 16 stuffed dates

½ cup whole milk ricotta

1 tablespoon sugar

1 teaspoon finely chopped lemon zest

12 whole raw almonds, finely chopped

½ teaspoon orange blossom water (optional)

16 dates, preferably medjool

8 whole raw almonds, cut in half lengthwise, for garnish

In a bowl, combine the ricotta with the sugar, lemon zest, chopped almonds, and optional orange blossom water. Mix well with a fork to blend ingredients. Set aside.

Make a lengthwise slit in each date without cutting all the way through. Carefully open each date and remove the pit. Stuff the ricotta mixture into the dates, re-form the dates around the filling, allowing some of the ricotta filling to show through the slit, and smooth the top. To garnish, push an almond half, lengthwise, into the exposed ricotta filling of each date.

Arrange on a platter and chill until the ricotta firms up, about 1 hour. The dates can be made a day in advance. Keep refrigerated until ready to serve.

Rose-Scented Ricotta Cream

This ricotta dessert, perfumed with rose water, can be spooned into small goblets, but it looks especially beautiful served unmolded on a platter, the creamy white surface studded with almonds, dark chocolate, and translucent candied citrus peel. **Makes 10 servings**

Two 15-ounce containers whole milk ricotta

½ cup sugar

½ cup shelled, freshly toasted almonds, chopped

¼ cup finely diced candied orange peel, citron peel (page 113), or a combination of both

¼ cup chopped bittersweet chocolate

2 tablespoons rose water

Candied citrus peel and almonds for garnish, optional

With a dish underneath to catch the liquid, place the ricotta in a colander lined with cheesecloth, tie the cheesecloth over the top, and place a weight on top. Refrigerate ricotta and let drain overnight.

Beat ricotta until smooth and fluffy. Stir in the remaining ingredients until evenly incorporated. Chill until needed. Spoon into goblets and serve. To shape the mixture, use a metal skewer to poke holes in the bottom of a 32-ounce cottage cheese container. Line with cheesecloth. Pack ricotta mixture into the container and tap firmly against a wooden counter to settle the ingredients. Place container in a colander with a dish underneath and refrigerate until ready to serve.

Unmold and gently remove the cheesecloth. The mixture will be soft but will have the imprint of the cheesecloth on it and should maintain the shape of the container. If desired, you can garnish the top with additional candied fruits and almonds.

Mascarpone and Gorgonzola "Ice Cream" with Walnuts

This savory Italian "ice cream" is simple to prepare and so delicious that you'll be tempted to keep licking your fingers and the spatula as you work. Fortunately, that's the prerogative of the cook.

It is a delightful and unexpected way to serve cheese at the end of a meal. Look for *dolce latte* Gorgonzola, young, creamy, and fresh-tasting.

Makes 6 servings

4 ounces (about ½ cup) *dolce latte* Gorgonzola

8 ounces (about 1 cup) mascarpone

½ cup walnuts, finely chopped

½ cup heavy cream, whipped

In a bowl, cream together the Gorgonzola and mascarpone. Blend in the walnuts. Gently fold in the whipped cream.

Line a 15-ounce plastic container with cheesecloth, allowing some to extend over the top. Spoon in the cheese mixture and gently bang the container bottom on the counter to settle the ingredients. Cover with the remaining cheesecloth.

Place in the freezer for several hours, until firm. Unmold and peel off the cheesecloth. Serve with bread and/or crostini and a basket of fresh fruits. Grapes, pears, or figs go especially well with this "ice cream."

Confections

Giardinetto *Giardinetto* is Italian for little garden. For a dessert offering that is both simple and inviting, serve an assortment of confections and cookies, purchased from high-quality sources or homemade. Confections can be made in advance and kept in the pantry for months, ready to serve when needed.

Arrange the candy and cookies on a tray, surrounded by small fresh fruits and nuts. It will look as pretty and charming as a little garden in bloom. Following is an example of what your garden might look like:

Marzipan (page 118)

***Cotognata*, a quince candy (page 116)**

Strips of Candied Citrus Peel (page 113)

***Torrone*, Italian nougat, available at Italian specialty stores**

Individually wrapped chocolates, such as Baci chocolates imported from Italy

Cookies, homemade or purchased from a bakery

Small whole fruits of the season, such as cherries, figs, and apricots

Shelled nuts, such as walnuts and almonds

Place a paper doily on a tray or platter. Arrange the candies and cookies on the doily and garnish with fruits and nuts.

Chocolate-Covered Stuffed Dried

Figs Stuffed with toasted nuts and candied peel, and with a coating of bittersweet chocolate, the humble dried fig is elevated to a delectable, sophisticated confection that is easy to prepare.

Cutting through one of these confections reveals a mosaic of dark chocolate, a constellation of tiny fig seeds, toasty brown nuts, and translucent orange peel. Add to that the fascinating play of textures and flavors, and you'll find it almost impossible to eat only one. I should know, since I ate more in a short space of time than I'm willing to admit! **Makes 20**

¼ **cup whole unpeeled almonds**

¼ **cup walnut halves**

¼ **cup finely diced candied orange peel (page 113)**

Small pinch cinnamon, optional

20 small, moist, plump dried figs

6 ounces dark chocolate

Spread the nuts on a cookie sheet and toast at 350°F for 12 to 15 minutes, or until lightly browned. When cool, chop the nuts. Place in a bowl with the candied orange peel and optional cinnamon, and mix to distribute the ingredients.

continued

111

Cut the tough stems off the figs and split them in half lengthwise without cutting all the way through. Stuff a little nut mixture into each fig and re-form the fig, making sure that it holds its shape by pressing the cut ends together. Cut the chocolate into medium-sized squares. Place in a heatproof bowl over gently simmering water, making sure the water doesn't touch the bottom of the bowl. (Chocolate burns easily, so it needs careful attention.) Stir frequently with a wooden spoon. The chocolate is ready when it softens and is warm to the touch, not hot.

Dip 1 fig at a time into the chocolate, rolling it around with a toothpick until it is completely coated. Spear the fig with a toothpick and lift it out, letting excess chocolate drip off. Place on a baking sheet lined with waxed paper and let sit at room temperature. The candies are ready when the chocolate hardens completely.

Candied Citrus Peel

Candied citrus peel plays a role in many of the desserts in this book. Chemically colored and preserved candied fruit is a travesty of the authentic product. If this has been your only experience, it may be difficult to overcome your bias against candied fruit, and I don't blame you.

But once you taste true candied citrus peel, glowing and translucent as stained glass, with an almost jellied texture, deeply flavored and aromatic, you'll be converted.

There are also two alternatives to making your own candied peel. Purchase candied orange peels, packed in jars with syrup, in Middle Eastern markets. Lift the large pieces of peel out of the syrup and let them drain, then dice them as needed. Or buy good-quality orange marmalade and strain out the pieces of candied peel. These are good for baking, but not for serving separately as a confection.

Candied citrus peel keeps indefinitely; the sugar acts as a natural preservative. **Makes about 75 pieces**

continued

2 large thick-skinned oranges, 3 thick-skinned lemons, or 1 thick-skinned grapefruit, preferably organic

3 cups water

2¼ cups sugar

Juice of 1 orange, 1 lemon, or ½ grapefruit, depending on peel being candied

Sugar for coating citrus strips

Wash the fruit well. Score the fruit in quarters and peel off the rind. Put the peels in a bowl of water to cover, and weight down the peels with a plate so they are completely immersed. Soak for 2 days, changing the water once. Drain peels and cut into strips that are 2 inches long and about ¼ inch wide.

In a saucepan, stir together water and sugar. Bring to a boil over medium heat and boil until the sugar dissolves and the mixture is clear, about 30 seconds. Remove from the heat and let cool.

In a stainless steel saucepan, combine the sugar syrup, citrus strips, and juice, and bring to a boil over medium-high heat. Reduce the heat to very low and cook very slowly for 1 to 1½ hours, or until the water evaporates and the syrup thickens. The syrup is at the correct thickness when the surface is covered with bubbles. Be careful not to overcook the syrup or the sugar will crystallize. The peel should be tender to the bite and look translucent.

Drain in a colander. Spread the strips out on waxed paper or parchment paper, separating the individual strips. Let cool.

For the sugar coating, place sugar in a bowl and toss a few strips of peel at a time in the sugar until well coated. Shake off excess sugar.

Store in a tin or airtight glass jar.

Desserts and Sweet Snacks

Quince Fruit Candies

Cotognata is the Italian name for a candy made from a puree of quince cooked with sugar and lemon. Easy and fun to make, these amber-colored fruit candies sparkle in their sugar coating.

Wrap the candies in twists of waxed paper and serve on a pretty plate. *Cotognata* makes a delicious and wholesome addition to Giardinetto (page 108). **Makes a plateful**

1½ pounds fragrant, deep yellow quince

½ lemon, sliced

⅔ to 1 cup sugar plus extra for coating

Almond oil or mild vegetable oil

Place the quince and lemon in a pot with enough water to cover over high heat. Bring to a boil and cook until the quince is tender. Drain. Cut away the core and seeds. Cut the quince into chunks and put through the coarse screen of a food mill.

In a medium saucepan, stir together the quince and ⅔ cup sugar. Cook over medium heat, stirring occasionally. When mixture starts to thicken, taste for sweetness and add sugar as needed. Stir mixture constantly until quince puree pulls away from pan and looks glossy and translucent.

Spread on a lightly oiled large plate to a ½-inch thickness. Let cool. Cover with cheesecloth and leave in a dry place for 2 days. Turn the paste over and dry 1 additional day.

Cut paste into squares, strips, or diamonds. Dredge in sugar and shake off excess. Wrap each candy in a small piece of waxed paper and twist ends to seal. Do not refrigerate. Store in a tin or airtight glass jar.

Homemade Marzipan

Handcrafted marzipan is a world apart from the kind bought commercially. The homemade product, moist and textured, lets the taste of fresh almonds come through. Even if you think you hate marzipan, you may want to try this recipe just once. It might change your mind.

You can vary the basic recipe by adding flavorings such as coffee and rum, adding extra ground almonds to achieve the correct consistency. A little grated lemon zest kneaded into the almond marzipan is also delightful. Add marzipan to confections in Giardinetto (page 108). Makes ½ pound

1 cup sugar

½ cup water

1½ cups almonds, peeled

½ teaspoon almond extract

¼ teaspoon vanilla extract

Powdered sugar

In a saucepan over medium-low heat, boil together the sugar and water until a thick syrup forms, about 10 minutes. Let cool.

Grind the almonds in a nut grinder or hand-cranked cheese grater. Place in a bowl.

Add about ¼ cup of the cooled sugar syrup to the ground almonds, or enough to form a paste. Reserve the remainder for another use. Mix in the almond and vanilla extracts. Knead briefly on a surface sprinkled with powdered sugar. Roll into a sausage shape, wrap in waxed paper, and refrigerate until needed. Marzipan can be kept refrigerated for months.

To serve, cut into rounds or roll into balls and sprinkle with powdered sugar. Place in paper candy cups.

Page numbers in bold indicate illustrations.

A

Acaya dessert, 4, **5**

almond(s):

in Aunt Ida's famous cookies, 68, **69**

and carrot cake, 56–57

in chocolate and espresso cake, **46,** 47–48

in chocolate-covered stuffed dried figs, **110,**
111–112

in chocolate peaches, 20–21

and chocolate stuffing, fresh figs with, 16, **17**

in coppa barocca, 82

in dates filled with sweetened ricotta,
100–101

in homemade marzipan, 118–119

in orange blossom ice cream, 78

in ricotta soufflé, **58,** 59

in ricotta with cocoa and brandy, **92,** 93–94

ricotta with honey and, 95

in rose-scented ricotta cream, 102–103

in sweet spaghettini torta, 49–51, 50

apple(s):

baked, with Italian pudding, **32,** 33–34

panino, warm, **10,** 11

apricot preserves in warm apple panino, **10,** 11

apricots:

in coppa barocca, 82

in tender fruit and rum cake, 60–61

B

blackberries and panna, 21

blood oranges in orange liqueur, 18–19

brandy, ricotta with cocoa and, **92,** 93–94

bread:

and chocolate, 6

rough, with wine and sugar, **2,** 3

sweet olive oil quick, 62, **63**

brioche, whipped cream–filled, 84, **85**

bruschetta:

cherry, 30, **31**

with mascarpone, sweet, 12

C

cakes, 45–63

carrot and almond, 56–57

chocolate and espresso, **46,** 47–48

Italian rice, 52–53

ricotta soufflé, 59

semolina, **54,** 55–56

sweet olive oil quick bread, 62, **63**

sweet spaghettini torta, 49–51, **50**

tender fruit and rum, 60–61

candied citrus peel, 113–114, 115

in giardinetto, 108, **109**

candied orange peel:

in chocolate-covered stuffed dried figs, **110,**
111–112

in coppa barocca, 82

in Italian rice cake, 52–53

in rose-scented ricotta cream, 102–103

in semolina cake, **54,** 55–56

candies, quince fruit, 116–117

cantaloupe, 9

crostata, **64,** 65–66

in summer fruits with rose water and lemon,
25

carrot and almond cake, 56–57

celery, in sweet mineral juices, 8

cheese, 91–105

dates filled with sweetened ricotta, 100–101

goat, fresh figs with mint and, 96, **97**

mascarpone and Gorgonzola "ice cream"
with walnuts, **104,** 105

pears with mascarpone, **98,** 99

ricotta soufflé, **58,** 59

ricotta with cocoa and brandy, 92, 93–94

ricotta with honey and almonds, 95

rose-scented ricotta cream, 102–103

sweet bruschetta with mascarpone, 12

sweet spaghettini torta, 49–51, **50**

cherry(ies):

bruschetta, 30, **31**

in fruit bowl Lido San Giovanni, 7

chocolate:

and almond stuffing, fresh figs with, 16, **17**

in Aunt Ida's famous cookies, 68, **69**

bread and, 6

-covered stuffed dried figs, **110,** 111–112

and espresso cake, **46,** 47–48

peaches, 20–21

in rose-scented ricotta cream, 102–103

watermelon and, **28,** 29

in watermelon ice, 89–90

in watermelon "pudding," 40–41

citrus peel, candied, 113–114, **115**

cocoa, ricotta with brandy and, **92,** 93–94

confections, 107–119

candied citrus peel, 113–114, 115

chocolate-covered stuffed dried figs, **110,**
111–112

in giardinetto, 108, **109**

homemade marzipan, 118–119

quince fruit candies, 116–117

cookies, 68–73

Aunt Ida's famous, 68, **69**

in giardinetto, 108, **109**

hazelnut and lemon meringues, 73

cookies (continued)

    ladyfingers, **70,** 71–72

coppa barocca, 82

crostata, cantaloupe, **64,** 65–66

crust, Italian pastry, 66–67

currants, in baked apples with Italian pudding,

    32, 33–34

custard, rum, 37

D

date(s):

    filled with sweetened ricotta, 100–101

    shake, 88

    in tender fruit and rum cake, 60–61

E

escarole, in sweet mineral juices, 8

espresso:

    and chocolate cake, **46,** 47–48

    gelatina di, 42, **43**

F

fennel:

    in Acaya dessert, 4, **5**

    in sweet mineral juices, 8

figs:

    chocolate-covered stuffed dried, **110,**

        111–112

    fresh, with chocolate and almond stuffing,

        16, **17**

    fresh, with goat cheese and mint, 96, **97**

    in tender fruit and rum cake, 60–61

fruit(s), 14–34

    bowl Lido San Giovanni, 7

    summer, with rose water and lemon, 25

    tender, and rum cake, 60–61

    see also specific fruits

G

gelatina di espresso, 42, **43**

gelatins, *see* puddings and gelatins

giardinetto, 108, **109**

goat cheese, fresh figs with mint and, 96, **97**

Gorgonzola and mascarpone "ice cream" with

    walnuts, **104,** 105

grapefruit:

    in candied citrus peel, 113–114, **115**

    pink, dessert, 26, **27**

H

hazelnut and lemon meringues, 73

honey, ricotta with almonds and, 95

honeydew:

    ice cream, pink, **76,** 77

    in summer fruits with rose water and lemon,
        25

I

ice, watermelon, 89–90

ice cream, ice cream fantasies, 75–88

    coppa barocca, 82

    date shake, 88

    mascarpone and Gorgonzola, with walnuts,
        104, 105

    Mediterranean surprise, 86–87

    orange blossom, 78

    pink honeydew, **76,** 77

    rum, 79

    sandwich, open-face, **80,** 81

    strawberries Villa Borghese, 83

Italian pastry cream, 36

Italian pastry crust, 66–67

Italian pudding, baked apples with, **32,** 33–34

Italian rice cake, 52–53

J

juices, sweet mineral, 8

K

kiwi, in fruit bowl Lido San Giovanni, 7

L

ladyfingers, **70,** 71–72

lemon(s):

    in blood oranges in orange liqueur, 18–19

    in candied citrus peel, 113–114, **115**

    and hazelnut meringues, 73

    in quince fruit candies, 116–117

    summer fruits with rose water and, 25

lemon marmalade in open-face ice cream
        sandwich, **80,** 81

M

marzipan, homemade, 118–119

mascarpone:

    and Gorgonzola "ice cream" with walnuts,
        104, 105

    pears with, **98,** 99

    sweet bruschetta with, 12

Mediterranean surprise, 86–87

meringue(s):

    Aunt Ida's famous cookies, 68, **69**

    hazelnut and lemon, 73

R

raisins:

   in sweet olive oil quick bread, 62, **63**

   in tender fruit and rum cake, 60–61

raspberries in Moscato wine, 24

rice cake, Italian, 52–53

ricotta:

   with cocoa and brandy, **92,** 93–94

   cream, rose-scented, 102–103

   dates filled with sweetened, 100–101

   with honey and almonds, 95

   soufflé, **58,** 59

   in sweet spaghettini torta, 49–51, **50**

romaine lettuce, in sweet mineral juices, 8

rose-scented ricotta cream, 102–103

rose water, summer fruits with lemon and, 25

rum:

   in baked apples with Italian pudding, **32,**
      33–34

   cake, tender fruit and, 60–61

   custard, 37

   ice cream, 79

S

sandwich, open-face ice cream, **80,** 81

savoiardi (ladyfingers), **70,** 71–72

semolina cake, **54,** 55–56

shake, date, 88

soufflé, ricotta, **58,** 59

spaghettini torta, sweet, 49–51, **50**

strawberries Villa Borghese, 83

sugar, rough bread with wine and, **2,** 3

T

tangerines, in Acaya dessert, 4, 5

torta, sweet spaghettini, 49–51, **50**

W

walnuts:

   in chocolate and espresso cake, **46,** 47–48

   in chocolate-covered stuffed dried figs, **110,**
      111–112

   in fresh figs with goat cheese and mint, 96,
      97

   in Italian rice cake, 52–53

   mascarpone and Gorgonzola "ice cream"
      with, **104,** 105

watermelon:

   and chocolate, **28,** 29

   ice, 89–90

   "pudding," 40–41

whipped cream–filled brioche, 84, **85**

wine:

   Moscato, raspberries in, 24

   red, in cherry bruschetta, 30, **31**

   red, peaches in a glass of, **22,** 23

   rough bread with sugar and, **2,** 3